Time is a Bright Light

By Nim Barnes

Published by New Generation Publishing in 2016

Copyright © Nim Barnes 2016

First Edition

The author asserts the moral right under the Copyright, Designs and Patents Act 1988 to be identified as the author of this work.

All Rights reserved. No part of this publication may be reproduced, stored in a retrieval system or transmitted, in any form or by any means without the prior consent of the author, nor be otherwise circulated in any form of binding or cover other than that which it is published and without a similar condition being imposed on the subsequent purchaser.

www.newgeneration-publishing.com

Time is a Bright Light

The road home from Sands - where the trees part
And the tarmac falls away down the long hill,
The morning flies to meet you on pale blue wings;
And you know, in that moment, that gravity is transient.
The down-pull is cheating you ... you can fly ... fly ...
Part of you need not stay in the car, meandering home,
Surging feeling under the ribs, and you could be free ...
nearly...

What would you know then? One with the dawn air
And the feeling of infinite space, the tugging certainty
That there is not an end, nor a wall, nor an edge to
anything....
Away from the discipline of sun-orbit, earth-control.
Time is a bright light. A huge revolving light
Measuring our night and day, season and tide,
Year and century. We record them. The revolutions
Mark their way. Mark our way, birth to death,
Earth-wombed person, time-allotted, sun-controlled.

Beyond the sun's rule, what then? - Eternity.
Released from ageing, measuring, discipline;
Unleashed from the hold of the flame-planet that is time,
Free from the gripping hand of gravity, the weight
Of body-shackles, the limitations to travel,
The frustrations of edge-flesh, the inability to merge
As spirit to spirit merges in empathy, ignoring space.
(And prisoned minds as limited as the confines of the
skull,
Receive and reject, the unfledged soul cannot fly.)

Time is but a bright light, horizons are not real,
Gravity is a stranglehold, infinity is as the air.
Human needs for sleep and food are a discipline,
As is the inadequacy of bone-locked brain

Unable yet to hold the thought of endless, space, time,
And all the connotations of limitless beauty
And as yet unfelt depths of thought and feeling.
The embryo ghost is encased by an earth-tamed mind.

Only in love are we light-free, spirit wild.
God of Love, have I seen You then on the wings of the morning?
Where the trees part, and the view is over the edge of the world,
And the sky is full of a dream we have yet to dream?

The Single Sperm

What a very religious lot, they are, the disbelievers.
Convinced in their narrow, unopened intellects
That the world must run on its rails stick to the book,
Progress only in the appointed way, from the dawn
                of the first day
To the end of time. Relentless, ordered, undeviatable plan,
Nothing unusual must happen. Not a single sperm.

It couldn't have happened! A wild sperm!
Straight from the Source of all creation!
(Well, who created all sperms, everywhere,
And every living cell in the entire universe?)
That you should create one tiny miniscule wild sperm
Outside the day to day order of things - (Your own order!)
A very religious bunch, the Disbelievers.

But, it wasn't a wholly human, finite sperm
That begat You a son who could walk across the sea,
Whose rays could heal a wound, or calm a wild colt,
Turn water to wine, or make bread from thin air.
That vibrant psi that cured insanity,
Flowed strength into the paralysed where they lay,
Absorbed the storm and laid the sea to rest,..........
What mortal phallus sired a Son like Yours?
We, who can't stop a draught across the floor,
Or ease our dear ones with the common cold.

I hope there was a moment once in time
Of pure, unearthly, all-transcending joy
In which you passed Your world Your perfect Son;
(Against which all our passions are candle-flames,
Comparing their minuteness with the sun.)

Forgive us, Lord, for being so religious
We mistake You for a very hidebound god.

Teach us the rhythms we feel are for <u>our</u> smallness,
The word to guide the world into the way,
Show us how light-wild, limit-free You are,
Let us applaud Your many million miracles,
And know He was Your Son, - and He was Beautiful.

The Sea

A pale evening, a very grey sea, restless.
Endless motion, light breaking up dark, grey shattering light,
White sun and restless water. I must be alone at the edge of it,
Feeling the wind, feeling the sea, part of it,
Feeling the sky - cloud tides like drifting music,
Over it all the feel of music - surging, falling, flowing.
Breaking, advancing, retreating - living water,
Pulled in by the moon, alive with floating sun.
Liquid sky full of white light, and just me on the sand,
Part of it. Living water in me. Flood-tide. Restless, wanting,
Wanting what? To be one with the beauty, one with the feeling
Have it all inside me, endlessly, surging,
pulling...pulling...pulling...

What will relieve it? What will be enough to fulfil?
Not loving your man, although you flow like the sea,
Time and again, and call him again, man's love is not enough.
To fill up the longing of so much beauty it must be more,
It must be walking forward to the edge of death again
With a new life. It must be filling up to the heaviness
And aching fullness, it must be living down the pain all over you
Bearing against the pain, opening your body, like opening your soul,
And feeling the love, the love that is like sea-feeling
All over you, moving, rushing, surging, filling the secret voids with joy.

I must be down by the sea for the whole beauty, God-Longing.

If I had no man, it would make me want a man,
But loving a man I am further involved with the sea and the sky
Doors open wide, and passing through I see a new horizon,
Beauty calls, relentless, calls me on, plays me
Like a violin string - hard ache down to my knees,
There will be no peace until my body has opened and given again,
Till the baby is tugging the milk out through my breasts,
And all the longing is breaking free in tenderness.

The Larch

Electric green of April larch, sight-calling -
Amid the dry storm-splintered stems of winter bracken,
And funeral garb of pine; - virile, spring-thrilling,
Needles moist in the sun, as new as the morning.

Obvious as a singing bird or a naked body,
Or an open flower with dusty stamens, scenting,
Vibrant, dawn-wakening, spring-happy perfect green
Still in the quiet air, speaking with Love Himself.

Lord, let my sons grow wild and straight as the sapling larch,
Each in their unique way, as You designed them,
To love to their ultimate depth and sensitivity
With all the purpose and strength You placed within.

Let them not be self-orientated when grown men,
Restless for their own comfort as babes in arms,
But let them grow upward and outward, caring, protecting,
Living to bring forth joy as the April larch.

Let them be sure of their power as the bliss-drunk bird,
Throbbing and thrilling above in the topmost bough.
Let them not feel that to force the notes in winter
Will fit them the better for answering the call of spring.

Let them feel free as the chaffinch immersed in his building
Making his stronghold inviolate with shreds of moss,
Impervious to the panic of creed or fashion,
Sure of their way as the swallows crossing the sea.

Let them know freedom means following close to the call of love,
Giving your all, for all to be given to you,

Let them not ever confuse freedom with madness,
Which is fumbling to guide the soul with a groping mind.

Let them be honest as the open flower to the questing bee,
Hurt not other's dreams, crushing their bloom in bud;
Let them be true to the roots of the love from which they sprang,
And sure in their truth as the green of an April larch.

The Feeling

It's sun on leaves, really, that is the most tangible of all,
Sun on white bark, or moving leaves flustered by the wind,
Or sun on a quiet sea, a distance of liquid diamond
And mist-vague morning; or sun on snow.
Nothing, no nothing, is quite so perfect as sun on snow.
The world held in trance, light beautiful, shadow-stilled,
Beneath a spell. Then, yes, the Feeling is alive,
To be held, held in every living cell, kept close.

John says, "In the Beginning was the word..."
But before the word, surely, there was the Feeling-
In a firmament strewn with stars like a field of buttercups,
And clouds flowing like rivers across the moon-
The Feeling that is the music of the mind,
This we must seek, keep alive, this we must love,
If this is all we can reach as yet, this we must know,
Let there be sun on the summer grass, Lord,
                    Let there be light.

The Dream

What are You but a dream? The Endless Dream,
The Light that shines in the darkness? The endless Light.
The dream of blossom liquid in the bough,
Moist promise of daffodils in earth-bound bulbs,
Of virile salt-rich succour in the earth,
Of summers live kaleidoscope in spring,
The gentian-canopied morning in the dawn,
All dreams of drawing forward in the air.

If it were not for Dreams - no surging spring,
No singing thrush, no swinging round the sun,
No suckling litters, no fish-haunted pools,
No fruiting tree, no tide, no fire, no love.

The Dream of Life - and more, the Unfelt Power,
That draws us on, despite black cynicism,
Of groping mind; or backward turning psi
Peevishly seeking womb-like sanctuary,
Lacking the courage to respond to You.

But You are patient, - still the seasons turn,
The field shoots green, the eggs lie in the nest.
The mystic evening call still rapes the mind
Till turgid souls find intercourse with You
Steeped in the wine of perfect love - amazed
As waves of silent music calm the heart.

When shall we learn to live as You decree?
To outgrow self, and love until the soul,
Flowing to other souls, becomes as light
That leaves the body's star; as pinpoint sparks
In the wide bowl of black infinity
Travel a million light-years seeking out
White oceans of still waters in the moon.

Re Matthew 10.29.31

Little decomposing scrap of feathered dust,
Two ounces of ecstasy and courage, dust to dust,
It won't be long before you are dust again.
Let me cover you with pine needles under your own trees.

For these are your woods - here you sang and loved,
With shrill sharp notes you pricked the sky awake
And gave another minute heart your life -
Did you have to fight for her favours, you fierce and
valiant handful?

Here you searched, foraged, made your nest secure, -
They relied on you. You, whom the wind could blow
away,
In blistering heat or storm - wild rain, you had dignity.
With aching wings you did not seek release, you would
have scorned to.

How cruel fire-cold teeth of winter frost
Must have burnt deep to bite your gasping lungs,
But when the sky gave birth to spring again
We only heard the love-flow in your song.

Was it some vile insecticide that killed you?
What arrogant obtuse intelligence
Gave agony to you - who loved so stridently
We stood to feel our hearts lift up with yours.

We should have learned from you - had we been wise,
To sing and love and patiently endure,
Lord, give us humility and truth to tell him,
"You are of more value than many of _us_!"

Prayer

Give me strength, Oh Lord,
To be annoyed and not to give back,
To be snubbed and not to wilt,
To be ignored and not to be depressed,
To be laughed at and not to be put out,
To feel tired or ill and not to be a bore.
    Give me the strength of a rock,

Give me energy, Oh Lord,
To carry my burdens with a straight back,
To do another's chore and not to notice it,
To be without sleep and use the hours to good account,
To be infected but to heal myself,
To know anxiety and not to feel weary,
    Give me the energy of a flood-tide.

Give me vision, Oh Lord.
To know the power of prayer and remember to use it,
To hold steady to the Divine Instinct in the hurricane of life,
To replenish from Your Infinite mercy when humans fail me,
To open the shutters of my mind to the beams of Your sun,
To know that hell is only the pressure of disintegrated thought waves,
To draw from You the wisdom to absorb and re-arrange them,
    Give me vision like the daybreak.

Give me love, Oh Lord,
To understand another person's point of view,
To feel their fear and pain in me, as keenly as they do,
To receive with tenderness what they wish to uncover,
To help them cover what they wish to conceal,
To give the succour they need to fill them with strength,

To help them to find the safe way back to You,
To go with them all the way along their road,
   Give me love like infinity,
               Love like You, Lord.

November Night

Beyond the window, squares of blue-black night
And motionless silhouette of winter oak
Soon to be lost - dark floating into dark.
Night joining up the shadows of the room,
Black hole of the tree one with the black infinity,
All shapes fading, melting, merging...invisible,
With feelings merging, as water to water, oak and self.

The winter suspension, the quiet time, waiting:
Dream of spring in the tree, dream of child in me.
Root-spread, earth-certain, indestructible;
Sap-lively, bud ebullient, leaf-glorious;
Storm-withstanding, snow-enduring, steadfast.
As water to water, shade to shade, reach me.
Enter my soul the wisdom of an oak tree.

Every acorn a miniature testament, God-perfect.
Knowing the way to grow into an oak tree.
How to root, what to draw up, how to grow.
How to spread wide, how to endure, how to fulfil,
And bring forth again a million tiny acorns.

God, give to my child the wisdom of an acorn.
He's about that size now - make strong his instinctive knowledge
Of how his soul should grow - root him in Your love,
To draw up courage, vigour, selflessness,
Ready to spread his work, his help, his ability
As far as his strength will carry - farther each year.
Ready to bring forth love, where love is needed,
Ready to give all he has got to give.

Tonight while the oak and I are together in shadow flow,
Quiet so quiet this velvet star-blind night
Give to my son the fearlessness of the way,
Let him have, always, the wisdom of an acorn.

Motorway

More than the hours of preacher's exhortations,
More than revised or modernised translations,
Or stiff new books of Alternative praying,
To words we knew so well that in whose saying
We rumbled homewards to a loved abode...
Silent - they speak, the flowers beside the road.

Grey tarmac strips show man's effective might -
Nature demolished, this he deems his right.
Iron jaws soil, seed and life have savaged, lifted,
And concrete, rubble, stone and gravel shifted,
So never petal, leaf nor blade of grass
Shall stem our stern impetus as we pass.

Yet by dead ways, in this discarded dust
The seed is King! The shoot is upward thrust
The celandine lives! - and man is impotent.
Divine is pollen power and bee's intent
Creation lives, Love gives, as we pass by,
In yellow stamens laughing to the sky.

Matins

I believe in God, Father Almighty - do I?
You seem certain. But I believe in love, yes.
I am a woman, I must believe in love.
The pattern and the plan, the living water,
The need for sanctuary, the cry for body- warmth,
The love in the womb with child, the love in the breast,
Love for a man, for a child, for home, for friends;
If You are love, then I believe in You.

Maker of heaven and earth, and of all things visible
                             and invisible were they You?
They came into being very slowly I thought,
By a long evolving process - but was it You? - The process?
Were You the Thing invisible, the potential in the dust?
When the first living specks joined in love,
To create, to bring forth, to evolve - was it <u>You?</u>

Well, if not, was it all just a fluke - a mere chance
That it came into being - and if so, was it You? The Chance?
The Chance there was air to breathe and food to nourish,
Darkness for rest, and sun for warmth and growth -
The Chance to be, to grow, to live, to love,
Develop progress, create and love again?
The Chance they felt within the <u>need</u> to love,
The Chance they knew the Way - was that You?
Yes, I believe, He said that You are love,
And John the beloved said, You are the word.

But how like a <u>person</u> are You? Let me see this.
Are You just a great tidal wave of living love,
Rushing like water through our turgid souls
As spring sap rushes through the trees in March

Forcing the dream of blossom through the wood?
                      (And is <u>this</u> You?)

You, who believe in us, despite our inability,
Make us ponder upon the extent and range of the mind
That can create us, from two specks of dust.
We, who cannot create a blade of grass,
Could pause to wonder why we think <u>we</u> have a mind, a being,
Yet doubt if <u>You</u> have: Because we do doubt.

Give me, this day, the ability to understand
Why my tiny, idiot, poisoned, finite mind
Persists in seeing You as a dyspeptic old man,
With a long beard, wearing a brown dressing -gown
Heavily censorious, rather passed His prime-
And then in an outraged agony of disappointment
That You were so inconsiderate as to be so unlikely
                Peremptorily rejects You?
And can You, in your all-seeing wisdom and easy omnipotence
Watch me do this, again and again, and with infinite humour,
Forgive me even such crass banality as this?
Thank God, I am able to believe You can, and do.
Thank God, at least I am sure of that- Thank God,

              Thank You, Amen.

Love Story to Peter

What stopped the headache, the feeling of a lid on top of my brain,
A tight band round my throat, and the heavy air pressing inside my chest?
You did, and only you. What did you do? You loved me.

When you took me in your arms you took me inside yourself.
Shadow-walls grew round me, built a fortress from scorn,
A sanctuary from the arrows of indifference or anger.
You knew what I couldn't cope with, when I was beaten,
And you took me inside your shadow walls with tenderness.
Walls invulnerable, because invisible.
Only we knew of their existence, only we were aware.
I could take off my armour, and let my soul be naked to you.

And you, alive, came with your soul naked to me,
And trusted me with a love you could not retract.
Let all of your soul rush from your body, and flow into my soul,
So my loneliness melted inside to an agony of need for you.

Now, in the safety of your love, my soul opens to you,
You, who could never leave me and rend me in two
Like a torn garment; you who understand my dependency,
You, I need hide nothing from- this moment, I am totally vulnerable
Every sweet life-spring I have, flows to the fullness of my love,
Here, on the tide coming in are the waves of my trust and relief,

Breaking on the shores of your strength are the seas of my happiness,
From the warm living ocean of love that is my soul and yours.

January

The pine trees tower over one in weighty silence.
All around smells pungently of dank shadow-dark woods.
The air is like a green veil receding before one between the great trunks
The coldness is all inside one, there is no softness in winter shade,
Only a suspension of life, in a misty, inanimate waiting world.

The still greenness is broken by a spark of winter bird song!
Somewhere within the high sweep of near-black branch and needle
Thrums a heart the size of a snow-flake who believes in spring!
And suddenly the earth believes in rain-soft warmth and living sun,
The sky believes in high blue distances of shimmering haze,
And even ponderous conifers believe in little pine trees!

Hydon's Ball

The pine trees sweep the clouds with measured gestures
Dark trunks swaying to the wind in rhythmic trance
Iron roots taking the strain as these huge black trees
Bow and return with awesome dignity.

The sliding sky is wild with swishing pine needles
And there are You - and this is Your cathedral.
These massive trees and me, we are aware of You,
And every cell within us all lives from Your life.

Why do we seek You in the pale small print of
mistranslated word?
Why do we argue on You with the muddled mind of man?
When we can feel You in our sap and wood and blood and
bone.
And stand and hold You in our hearts in Your cathedral?

Genesis 1. 27

What is a boy? He is the one, who loves your gaiety,
Is proud of your body, your hands, your tidy waist-line,
The way you walk, the way your hair goes back,
Who shows you off to his friends, basks in their teasing,
Uncovers his dream-world, tells you all his truth,
Fills up with his tenderness, gives himself to you whole,
To make, damage or break, with caring or carelessness,
Lights himself on your flame, dies with your embers.
Believes in your wholeness, has faith in your abilities,
Trusts you to weather the storms, stand by his side,
Be beautiful, loyal, happy, cheerful always.
Floats on the sea of your love in the summer tide.

What is a man? He is the one who loves you through
dreariness
Feels for your hopelessness, failures, agonies,
Finds you torpid and sinking, heavy with broken dreams,
Dull in the stomach so petty with trivial woes,
Unreasoning temper keeping at bay despair.
Touches you with his hands, pulls up the tide in you.
With lips and hands brings back the ebbing flow,
Calls through your body the rush of what was lost to you,
Releases the love you couldn't feel was there.
Knows when the storms have taken, broken, drowned you.
Knows when it is a man has got to care.

Flu

A full head, and a bed hot with poison-heavy limbs,
And a limp body, breathing through the pain, wearily;
Sinking slowly through the mattress into the dark
                            space of mindlessness;
And through it all, the intermittent dream of the
                            lifting pull.
All that is one, rising slowly out of one's body
And hovering, motionless, like a smoke-cloud
                            over the embers.

Lifting out of the pain, out of the dizziness; with
                            the magnet
That holds one inexorably to this hulk of sickening flesh
Loosening it's hold just enough for one to feel the
                            lifting pull.
The lightness of the air and the dimming of the pain; no
reality -
But reflected in one's head a day-dream like reality,
A sight-dream in the mind, like fire in a red hot coal.

A dream of the smallness of this ball of earth and water,
Rotating with disciplined exactitude, in perfect orbit,
Swinging like some minute magnetized pin-head
In the silent blue-grey vastness of unending distance,
Swung by the same current from the sun, as ties me
Relentlessly to this breathing, beating, aching cage.

One escapes a little with the strong lifting pull,
In the same elastic way a tide of music
Draws the sensations beyond the body's grasp
In strands, cascades and colour-swirled floods of sound;
As the hard need can leap beyond the compass of the skin
Pulling the loneliness across the miles to touch one's lover;
As love enfolds the new-born babe with womb-like
shadow-walls,

And holds invisible threads of those he cares for;
So one escapes a little space of heavy hurting time.

And part of this fluid electric field of floating life
Alive above the bed in effortless trance-like freedom,
Is aware of the pull and hunger and strength of the
                                    ultimate life-flow
Aware that the end will be leaving go, in a sort of
                                    raw sanity,
Of the magnet that clamps the eye to a limited vision;
And a final reaching out by the soul for the vista of truth.

Evening

I am standing here on the edge of the wood, where the tree line ends,
Gazing at the unveiled sky, gazing at infinity.
At the end of the wood, at the end of today,
Where the view of the sky is not obscured by branches,
And the reaching out is not hampered by a morning-busy mind.

The day-spring that gave the living waters of today is lessening
Today has poured away down the sides of time,
The rushing, restless ever-changing streams,
The daytime's action, urgent thoughts of now,
Have given into the still waters of deep dreams.

The soundless music of the evening is over all the wood,
And over the field with the patchy new-born green of this week's wheat,
In the breathing of the leaves there is a quiet intensity
In the listening earth contentment, a peace,
The peace of God, which passes all understanding
And yet is understood - by the new wheat and by the ancient oaks.

And all the time the dark is coming down, coming down.
From the outer ends of the sky - which has no ending,
With the feel-less touch of God, it is coming down.
With the certainty that is only His, it will come.
The field and the woods will be filled up with the night,
In just a little while there will be a wordless guiding of the soul,
A hunger for home, a feeling-out for one's own place,
A going back - to bed, to love, to sleep.

Escape

What a beautiful day, - a day to escape!
A day to be up there with the wild birds
Somewhere between the tree line and infinity.

To leave one's body propped against a tree-trunk,
Dreaming sun-dreams with all the other trees,
Wondering what it feels like to have roots
Probing with hungry threads into the black interior
Drawing up life-specks into the sun-world,
Making little lime-juice-green leaves
With absolute precision, and timeless wisdom.

Leave it propped there, empty, with wide-open eyes,
Gazing at the black lace prison of a million tiny birch twigs,
Weaving shadow patterns to remind one, one is finite,
Earthbound. Gravity is a horizontal cage.

So what a perfect morning to float up to it all!
A pale sky, colourless behind the branches,
The lifting feeling- and then the white opaque brightness of spring
Forgiving winter for the love-silence of snow.

No tranquillity, a business of sap,
Every tree awake inside the immobility,
A rushing joy beneath the bark.
All the earth catching life from the sky,
And all infinity alive with sky music
And the singing of birds.

Dusk

There is something about looking at the roses as night is falling,
And the garden is quiet with the trance-like quiet of sleeping trees
That is very like floating one's waking thought on a river of music.

They are so still, the roses, when you come to them in a motionless dusk;
When all the birds are gathered home by the dying light.
And in a little while it will be too dark to distinguish the petals.

One almost expects them to fold their petals to sleep.
To resize or retreat, to cover or protect themselves in some way,
But they remain upright, open, frail, utterly at peace.

The darkness caresses them, the night air fills them,
As we turn to withdraw to our warmth and comfort
We leave them offering up their delicate perfection undismayed.

Later still, if one walks across the garden
When it is full of white light and standing shadows
And the dream-like chill that goes with the white light

If one stands beside the roses under the stars
There is a quality of wonder, like very rare music
In the fact that roses do not close their petals in the dark.

Devotions

Grey-cold cathedral atmosphere of subduing quality:
The soul retreats, and the disproportionate noise made by one's feet
Becomes a gross impertinence. Precisely pewed
One smells the dust and varnish smell through gloves in front of one's nose.
Stiff pile of hassock, hard line of pew edge, and praying - smell;
Looking up at the powerful lift of finely-fashioned stone,
From a long long way behind one's eyes,
One awaits, doubtfully, the stimulation of the spirit.

So. Try to feel this all was built with love - and sweat,
And discipline - and back ache - and ordered thought,
And earnest good intention from the heart
Flowing like water - though frozen hard by awe.
- And is a sanctuary for people's prayers - so one can kneel
And feel the thoughts and hopes and fears and faith
Of those who prayed before, and so one's stomach
Prays fervently, in empathy, for them; while one's mind doodles
With the odd phrase and thought thrown at one's feet
By the long waves of oft-repeated sound
Familiarity has made meaningless.

So. Try to realise all these dark red sounds
The organ makes are dreams of praise and joy
Written by those who loved Him more than you,
Which now repeats the rapture that they knew
In solemn beauty for the rest of time.
Who knows? The very notes may be the same
That startled shepherd lads that star-drenched night
The angels came to town in Bethlehem?

But, oh relief! And floodtide of the soul!

To see again the nearness of the sky!
The fingertips can touch infinity
Where man-built ceiling cannot come between,
Defiant daisy, smug-bright in the grass,
Where guillotine blade of mower failed to find,
Reminds how He creates with bliss-filled bee
And specks of yellow dust, small cheerful things
To lift the heart and brighten up one's dreams.

I thought how shoulder-weary, serious men
Gild roofs to please the maker of the sun, -
And when I saw two butterflies chase by
I felt as though I saw Him wink at me!

Conversation with a three-year-old

"When I'm a big man," said my smallest son,
"I'm going to drive a fire-engine, fast, fast,
And you can sit on top and ring the bell,
And we will go a hundred miles an hour!"

"I may be a bit old for it," I said.
"You won't feel old when we are going fast,
Because we will be going to a fire
To water it, and get the people out."

He had the essence there, my smallest son.
Self-orientation makes a soul aware
Of its own gaping, limp deficiencies.
In service to the world self-doubt should die;
Discarded as the disused husk of wheat,
And only the potential truth exist.

"Then, one day we will have a great big house,
With lions, and elephants, and rabbits even,
And they'll give rides to everyone who comes,
- Except the lions who might eat people up!"

"A trifle awkward that, " I said, "And who
Will feed the lions then on our day off?"
"We won't want a day off at all," he said,
"Because we'll love the lions, and they'll be <u>there</u>".

I took his point; there would be such rapport
The ultimate fulfilment would be found.
The world would proffer blandishments in vain,
Only in giving can we find contentment
He was in tune with life, my smallest son.

"And when you're very old, and I can read,
We'll sing the words in church out very loud,

And God will be surprised that I can read,
So He won't mind if I take all the hassocks,
And make a castle with them, will He then?"

"Well, <u>He</u> may not, but other people may,
One isn't meant to fidget during church".

"Well, I will wait till all those people go,
And only God and I are left behind.
Then we'll get all the hassocks in the church,
And build a huge great castle in the aisle,
So tall it reaches right up to the roof,
Then God and I will run and kick it down,
And we will laugh until our tummies burst!"

You know the harmony of brotherly love,
Co-operation, rich enjoyment shared,
Strength found in close affinity of minds.
I wish the world held many more like you,
You are so very wise, my smallest son.

Conversation with a thirteen year old

"What do you think of these chaps on the moon?"
Enquired my son, the day the news arrived.
 "Well," I said, "I don't know....
I think it's half a century too soon.
There seems a lot to tidy up down here
Before we start to take on outer space!"

"But it will come," he said, "and better now.
While we have men of calibre and power.
Sufficient to be equal to the task!"

"Oh it will come, I'm sure, in God's good time.
We will thrust forth and join with other worlds.
It seems the obvious enough progression
From what we find in nature on this globe.
I mean we know each human foetus grows
Through all the stages of evolving life,
And then the child matures to make the man,
In natural gradual process down the years,
Conquering skills and understanding self.
So evolution follows the same plan.
In our relationship with the Almighty
(At two the caveman, but by seven the man
Of the Old Testament, dependant
Still resistant often, petulant and stubborn,
But happiest while in obedience.)
So came man down the anno domini
Just the same way each human child matures.
Because they say our image of Him alters
With what we feel we need our God to be.
But the same way your views on Daddy and me
Have varied down the years?"
"Oh yes," he said,
"I realise now you're neither of you perfect:"
"That can't have taken very long," I said,

"But so it follows, we have reached today,
The age to question, criticise, reject,
Our Father, and the powers from within
Urge to thrust forth and reach for other worlds."

"Yes. I see what you mean," exclaimed my son,
"*This is the puberty of evolution!*
That's why there's so much power in the young.
Today we hold the feelings in ourselves
In tune with the vibrations of the world!
The moon shot is a sex experiment.
And Neil Armstrong in his rubber suit.
The first sheathed sperm to leave a virile world."

"Err, yes," I said, "you could put it like that!"

"When I grow up I'm going to design
Much the most powerful rocket ever made -
Of course, there'll be a multitude of problems
You wouldn't understand," explained my son.
"There are no near-worlds in this universe
That can alone support a human life."

"Perhaps," I said, "like many a patient pa
We'll give support until they learn to cope?"

"Oh no", he stated, "We now must go much further
Into a universe we can't yet see....
(One isn't meant to marry one's relations.)
With the resources of another planet;
For this world is the male, "asserted he.

"Quite, quite," I said. (I know when to agree.)

"We might have to bash on for aeons of time.
Travelling, possibly, passed the speed of light,
Frozen in packages like bird's eye peas.
Then we'd be slowly thawed through, on arrival,

By time-switch very carefully worked out."

"Let's hope they're wizards at arithmetic,
We might feel rather groggy going soggy,
In plastic cartons hurtling on through space;"

"Mummy, we'll have computers for all this",
Said he, with weary patience for the old.
"In any case you'd be most carefully wrapped
Or bits of you might rub off on the way!"

"Let's avoid breakage if we can," I said.

"Oh well, all this won't be until you're dead!
We'll first communicate with all the stars
In modern intergalaxian radio Morse,
(In case there's an indigenous population)
We'll bleep through space with friendly messages,
Our sperm must be received with happy welcome,
It wouldn't do to rape them with our rocket!"

"I must say, now, it all sounds rather fun!"

"Oh, more than fun! The most exciting thing
The world has dreamed of in its wildest dreams!
And I shall be the one," explained my son,
"So in a way it will be my brain-power,
And all my dreams that populated space!"

"Help!" I said, "Well the best of British luck!
But don't forget with all this brilliant science
A man needs also kindness, heart and love,
And softness with the weaker in the fold."

"Mummy!" he cried, "you keep on about luck,
And this whole project comes from God's own mind,
How the hell do you think we'd make first base
If we were not the sort of men He liked?"

Birth

Release, the pain is fading, the effort is over.
I am sore, limp, satiated and alive with an incredible ecstasy
Entirely dependent on the sight and sound and smell of another personality -
Who, very slippery and furious,
Is bellowing, and kicking tiny sticky legs
In impotent protest against the insides of my thighs.

What can I give you then that will be enough?
As soon as they let me, the colostrum from my breast-
There, then- with your impetuous hurting energy
Stimulate your birthright, empty me into yourself.
The fierce electric love-flow from my body
Invisible to finite eyes, but strong as radar beams
Pull it from every nerve to feed your soul.
With the inevitable tyranny of the wholly vulnerable
Make my mind a prisoner to your importunity.

What have you given me that makes this your world?
A filling-up with the life-drought as a tree fills up with sap
Without which there is no flowering or fruiting;
A ride on the extended wings of agony, to the edge of endurance
And a glance over the edge at the infinite purpose,
Somehow embodied now in you, - to hold in my arms,
To stroke your hair with my lips, to give my nipple to,
You, to love my love to, and feel it absorbed
With systematic intensity by your imperious necessity -
You little raw, damp, demanding bundle of naked need.

An Answer

Well yes, my love, I know, dear love, it isn't easy.
But then what is; if one feels or thinks at all, what is?

Look at it this way. If you were a mole
You wouldn't find it easy to believe in sparrows.
And if you were a sparrow, you wouldn't believe in tigers.
(Unless you were a sparrow that lived in a zoo.)
And if you were a tiger that lived in the jungle
You wouldn't believe in an English sahib unless you saw one.
And you'd never begin to believe in what went on inside: -
Worry over the government of the day, over income tax,
School fees, the Stock Exchange, promotion prospects,
You wouldn't begin, my intellectually limited friend.

But, something tells a tiger what to eat, and where to hunt.
Someone tells a sparrow how to make a nest,
On what to feed a fledgling. Someone knows
How mole mamas must care for baby moles.
Call it nature; call it instinct, I won't argue.
I am happy to worship the Force that prompts our Instinct,
That makes it the Natural Thing for there to be love,
Rather than starving fledglings screaming in endless chaos,
And I'll bet that if I have a mind, this Force has a greater one,
And I'm as grateful He has, as if I were a baby mole.

Again

A green silence, full of sun-shafts like white glass.
Rods of mist, leaning from branch to branch, motionless.
A silence one can feel with one's mind,
The leaves are not moving this morning.
The stillness is fact, like a melody - the desultory bird-song
Is the accompaniment to the hush, not an interruption.
Autumn light and still branches is sight-silence.
So long as the leaves don't move, Lord, I can feel again.

To my own tree, where the world is so full of leaves
There are no paths to the sky, and the light is captured
And held still, and given to one in a green silence.
And the bark has the same damp living roughness
Under one's hands it had a year ago, and the working roots
Hold to the same pattern they had a year ago,
And every leaf holds still for one this morning
And loves one with the sensitivity of God.

Because yesterday was a bad day, full of dry-ache tears,
Unwise words, and dying dreams, and fist-tight throat-pain,
And last night was a long black thinking-time on a grey pillow,
So today is a pale new plan, hatched from despair
A fledgling hope to be taken and let fly - gently,
On fragile, tentative wings - in a green silence.

Beyond

What lies beyond the nearness of our finite sight?
Where every star compares with nearness of a grain of sand,
Snatched from the desert wastes by one small fist.
And flung into the night. What lies beyond?

What sings beyond the eight fine notes of choral scale?
The disciplines of aural range confined to us,
In ear drum, nerve and brain and bone – what lies beyond?
What songs divine flood out, or sunrise paints the walls of space?

What scents and shades, what, vision clearing may we see?
Each separate jewel of dust-speck on an insects wing,
Each petals fragrance, dancing on the wind,
Each rainbow, made from bending light – what lies beyond?

God let me gaze at Your night skies and through the strands
Of liquid light that float like prayers across the moon,
In just one moment let me feel a promised hour,
And wonder with the trees and stars – Who lies beyond?

Then

When we are free from bonds of finite traits,
Shall we move forward with the speed of thought,
Think with the penetration of a dream?
(Where no horizons fake false boundaries.)
Released from the closed circuit of reaction
That is the range of flesh-imprisoned psi
         Shall we feel You?

When we can hear the colours as wind-wild music,
See sounds as waves and patterns in the air,
Feel that life-force that brings seedlings from the seed
Rush like a whirl-wind through the reaches of space
To place a pollen-speck – or flood the sunrise
Will half a million miles of liquid flame,
         Shall we be nearer You?

When we can hear and take in every human voice;
Realise the fears behind the unwise actions
The hopes, the heaving depths of all the day-dreams
When, softly, new awareness finds fresh tenderness,
Love's still response to need's unspoken prayer.......
When every thought is how to gently succour,
         Shall we know You?

When we can love by melding soul to soul,
When we can guide by touching mind to mind,
When we can love with love so pure and perfect
That every wave pulls in the tide of joy,
When we but try to love as Love loves us,
Then may we pass the impenetrable light?
         Then, shall we see You?

Indoors

The wind is making the trees make a noise like the sea tonight.
I wish I was a bird out there, and part of it all.
Our lives are so dull, because we are not part of the storm now

There is a roof between us and the sky,
A floor between us and the earth
We have built layers of comfort
Between this cold and gritty source of life,
And this rough, pounding billowing wild world.

The storms don't hit our faces with fierce rain-drops
And the earth doesn't bite deep chill into our feet

We are locked between ceiling and floor and wall-paper,
And our feelings are safe and dim.

But tonight when the stars are cold and sparkling,
The clouds are flowing like rivers, and the trees
Are crashing like the sea, I wish I were a bird,
Out there, part of it all, I think I would feel God.

Birdsong

Singing to the dark, toes curled round a black twig
Singing to the grey and singing to his love
Filling the wild space with her morning music,
Singing in the light sky, singing in her dawn.

Handsome feathers, flying wings, rejoicing heart.
Do we need to believe in angels? Were they ever there?
Do we need to read thin pages in a leather book?
Do we need to kneel on scratchy hassocks and implore?

We can listen to the ceremonies of the night.
Listen to the music of the darkness,
Singing out the stars, singing out the shadows,
Singing in her warm hours, singing in her apricot morning
Singing in her spring days, singing, singing, singing.

Moonlight

Translucent cloud, milk of the moon,
Traversing the silent sky, dreaming…..
The branches are still tonight, but the moving clouds
Caress the darkness with their flowing light.
And You show this to us.

And You have said "Come unto Me all ye
Who are heavy laden, and I will give you peace."
And no cruelty, no turmoil, no misery, no malice,
No agony can dim the moon, and nothing of man's
Can stem the Love, or challenge Your tranquillity
And You give this to us.

Nativity

Joseph…………..
Walking through the beginnings of night
Were you full in the stomach with worry and fright
Did it seem like a nightmare to be in this plight?
    Though you comforted her.

Joseph…………
Did you feel on the edge of despair?
Did you utter a curse, or beseech with a prayer
When no person in Bethlehem wanted to care
   …….and she so needed care.

When you led her at last through that strange stable door
Did you weep with relief as you swept up the floor?
Moved over the oxen and piled up the straw
    To make a bed for her.

Were you glad that the hours at the carpenter's table
Had made your arms strong, so you knew you were able
To carry her so carefully, in to the stable,
    And lay her down gently.

Joseph, did you cradle her head in your arms,
And wrap your cloak round her, to see she was warm,
Worry and fret if they'd both come to harm,
    Before the day dawned.

Did this all seem as though this could not have been planned,
As you knelt in the place where the oxen would stand,
And He entered this world with His head in your hand,
    And you cut His cord.

Did you lift Him to show her, did you wipe His Eyes?
- Did you suddenly both feel that blissful surprise
As He woke up old Bethlehem town with His cries
In the still night hours?

Did you find His swaddling bands – tell her to rest,
Did you help her to wrap Him, put Him to her breast?
Was it you who decided the manger was best
As a cradle for Him?

And then did you think it was strange as He lay
He filled the whole stable with light like the day
Or did you know, somehow, that this was the way
It would be now?

Did you go out and stand in the road, bathed in light,
Where His true Sires' star had set fire to the night
Was it wonder, fear, puzzlement, tenderness……or a
Loneliness you felt?

Had you just fed the donkey and unpacked the load,
When you heard up-raised voices outside in the road,
You'd just dimmed the lantern, - when in they all strode,
With their lambs and their noise!

Did He wake in the manger and cry in alarm,
Was Mary afraid it would all do Him harm,
Did you take Him and put Him again in her arm
For the comforting nipple?

Then the kings with their pomp – did you feel very grand,
Or did you find a place for the camels to stand,
Then water, then fodder – was there plenty to hand,
Or did you send out?

Did you kill a lamb – make a wrap from the fur,

Collect wood for the fire; cook the young meat for her
- Then, oh God what did you do with the myrrh –
Could you hide it from her?

When you dreamed of God's message that terrible night
Did you know in a moment you had to take flight?
Or wonder and worry if you'd get it right,
In the fitful hours?

Did you wonder if you would see your workshop again?
And how you would manage – no saw, lathe or plane,
And no place for shelter from sand-storm or rain,
And Him only 12 days old?

We take it as read you were able to provide,
Shelter, love, warmth, food, clothing and somewhere to hide,
And all that "was there until the death of Herod", implied,
In an inch of small print!

Joseph, the patience, the guts and the care
It must have all taken – thank God you were there
Or the Light of the World might have died in despair
In the oxen's stall.

The Light of the World – God sent Him to you
Like a little raw monkey, all wizened and new
Because you were a 'good man and just' and He knew
You were a loving man.

Luke 19.41

If Christ were standing here in Leicester Square
   -    The hair and the beard wouldn't look so out of place,
A few hippy clothes – Come to that I expect He is standing here!
Come to that I know He is. What does He feel?
       What do You feel my Lord?

You, whose touch was so deft, Whose hands so quiet
You took the colt! "Whereon yet never man sat"
And he went willingly into the shouting throng
Of milling people casting garments in the way –
Let us feel Your hands guiding us through the world this day.

Help us to know the rushing streams You send
Flood from the heart in full and perfect flow
When self-love dies, and in care for another
Our dearly loved one's bliss becomes our need.

You who with spit and clay restored the blind
Give us the inner sight to hate the false
And spread this gift; With deft and feel less touch
Rip off the scales from cold and tallow minds.

You, who with heaven-given authority,
Drove forth the money-lenders from His temple,
One humid evening in Jerusalem
Drive out this sickness from the cinemas now.

Dear Lord, when we move far away from You,
Be You, especially, closer still to us.

Winter

One day I shall die, and I hope I shall die unselfishly,
If I am in pain I hope I can hide it, God giving me courage,
I don't want horror, regrets or grief for those I love…..
But somehow we have made death difficult for people.

But tonight the woods have that unshaken hush of leafless branches,
While snowflakes, like miniature feathers flecked with silver,
Drift through the magical stillness, in snow-mirrored moonlight.
If I were a tiny furry animal, deep, deep in my sanctuary,
Barely breathing, curled tail-tight in moss warmed slumber
I think it would not be so hard to slip from sleep-drugged frailty
And just to emerge, nose quivering, tail whisking,
And blink black eyes at this world of mystic beauty
Where peace floats down to cover sleep with love.

So I hope my woods hold a million tiny furry ghosts
Cavorting blissfully in and out of the inky shadows
Who no longer need fear the predator's tooth or claw.
I'd love to see them and the birds – and hear the feathered choirs:
Where elation we sense as dawn creeps past the clouds –
And I hope they're all seen and heard by those earth-bound brothers
Whose footprint trails will intrigue the dogs tomorrow.

And sometimes I hope, on the days where I'm feeling bold,
I shall meet the white-robed monk with the lovely face
My daughter says, walks down the path behind the shrubbery

I hope we might find the support that I feel with the squirrels
But somehow we have made life complicated for people.

Sky

Passmore Street, unforgiving paving stones under tired feet and car smell,
London evening where the pavements seem to sweat dust,
And the smoke can't lose itself for the inertia of balmy air,
And all over one's being is seeking something that isn't there at all.

The reaching-out feeling that searches the evening mood
And finding only life-less brick, and stone, and glass windows
Returns to one, vibrating hard grey disappointed like discord
Traffic noise, outside one's head, hardly noticed;
High-walls-feeling inside one's chest, depressing, disillusioning;
And no knowledge of what it is one is feeling for.

Turning the corner on dull legs into Bourne Street;
A space in the houses, demolition's waste, a building site.
Space – view – however curtailed, however dreary.
Hectic relief in the chest, quite disproportionate, absurd.
But a view of translucent cloud above the house-tops
And somehow room to spread the soul like butter on bread!

Stop and look. Feel....... Suddenly evening-feeling like on the hills in Wales
In the rose garden in Suffolk, and on the sands by the sea,
The evening benefice, falling like rain, every nerve-head drenched.
In the certainty there is a very special sweetness at the end of the day,
A tranquil beauty that answers every call that lives on earth.

So I shall stand for a while where they have torn down walls,
Walls that keep the sky away, and will steep myself
In the gentleness in the air; depths of peace; (despite the passing turmoil.)
That comes as surely as the human need to love,

And touches the core of me with some immortal current,
That switches on the light for a little longer.

Then I must walk on briskly between the buildings again,
For if I stand here crying in the middle of Bourne Street,
The people that don't seem to feel the things that I feel,
Will stare at me and guess that I am potty!

Lightning Source UK Ltd.
Milton Keynes UK
UKOW02f1320021116
286691UK00003B/18/P